Those with wisdom, like Wanda Nash, win it the hard way, by winnowing their raw experience and beliefs till the full grains of truth emerge. We thank Wanda for her fearless and playful exploration of old age and death, which offers surprise, wonder and, to her delight and ours, breathing room.
Canon Roly Riem, Vice-Dean and Canon Chancellor, Winchester Cathedral

My abiding memory is of Wanda breathless in bed, oxygen tank by her side, mask in hand, surrounded by a group of twelve whom she led in reflection. Her decision to discontinue her chemotherapy in order to keep her mind clear during the final months of her life was characteristic, as was her determination, sense of fun and desire to serve her Lord. An inspiring example.
Eleanor Gordon RGN, Chemotherapy Nurse Specialist

The Bible Reading Fellowship
15 The Chambers, Vineyard
Abingdon OX14 3FE
brf.org.uk

The Bible Reading Fellowship (BRF) is a Registered Charity (233280)

ISBN 978 0 85746 558 0
First published 2017
10 9 8 7 6 5 4 3 2 1 0
All rights reserved

Acknowledgements
Unless otherwise stated, scripture quotations are taken from The Holy Bible, New
International Version (Anglicised edition) copyright © 1979, 1984, 2011 by Biblica.
Used by permission of Hodder & Stoughton Publishers, a Hachette UK company.
All rights reserved. 'NIV' is a registered trademark of Biblica. UK trademark number
1448790. • Scripture taken from the New King James Version®. Copyright © 1982
by Thomas Nelson. Used by permission. All rights reserved. • Scripture quotations
taken from the Amplified® Bible, Copyright © 1954, 1958, 1962, 1964, 1965, 1987
by The Lockman Foundation. Used by permission. (www.Lockman.org) • Scripture
quotations from The New Revised Standard Version of the Bible, Anglicised edition,
copyright © 1989, 1995 by the Division of Christian Education of the National Council
of the Churches of Christ in the United States of America. Used by permission. All
rights reserved. • Scripture quotations from Jubilee Bible 2000 (JUB), Copyright ©
2000, 2001, 2010 by Life Sentence Publishing, Inc. • Scripture quotations marked CCB
from the Christian Community Bible: Catholic Pastoral Edition (1st edition), London
St Pauls © 1988.

p. 5: 'SONbathe' by Jeanne Blowers, from The Call to Surrender. Used with kind
permission. • p. 82: 'Journey of Life' by Alvin Fine from Gates of Repentance © 1978,
revised 1996 by Central Conference of American Rabbis. Used by permission of the
Central Conference of American Rabbis. All rights reserved. • p. 84: 'We need to find
God' by Mother Teresa of Calcutta, reproduced with permission from the Mother
Teresa Centre (www.motherteresa.org).

Every effort has been made to trace and contact copyright owners for material used
in this resource. We apologise for any inadvertent omissions or errors, and would
ask those concerned to contact us so that full acknowledgement can be made in
the future.

A catalogue record for this book is available from the British Library

Printed and bound by CPI Group (UK) Ltd, Croydon CR0 4YY

COME, LET US AGE!

An invitation to grow old boldly

Wanda Nash

Edited by **Poppy Nash** and **Debbie Thrower**

NOT GETTING OLDER,

but

BEING OLD

– and my take on it

Wanda Nash's original title page

Contents

Acknowledgements

In preparing this book for publication, I am mindful of so many people who have influenced the contents, both directly and indirectly. Indeed, without their support much of this book would have remained on Wanda's computer as an unrealised manuscript.

It is an interesting challenge to write on behalf of another person. My mother would have wished to thank an extensive range of people for their contribution in shaping her thoughts, prayers and insights contained in this book. First and foremost, I believe Wanda would have heralded the unwavering support, love and companionship of my father, Archdeacon Trevor Nash, who journeyed alongside her in ageing and illness, coping with his own terminal illness as he did so.

A special vote of thanks must be given to my brother-in-law, Stan Roman, for his poignant illustrations, and to the Revd Tim Selwood, whose foreword so eloquently portrays my mother's outlook on life.

My three sisters, Lois, Phoebe and Jo, have been pillars of support in discussing our mother's encounter with ageing and illness, and in clarifying many memories of how she coped with her diminishing health. I would like to thank my husband Robin and sons Crispin and Gabriel for their understanding and patience through the evolution of the book.

And, of course, this book would never have got off the ground if it had not been for Debbie Thrower's enthusiasm, support and guidance. I am deeply appreciative of her contribution to the whole endeavour.

Poppy Nash

Foreword

I guess that, having enjoyed a friendship with Wanda for many years, I should not be surprised, in being asked to write this Foreword, that what follows is rather a 'lastword' from Wanda; or rather, a host of 'last words' from her deeply spiritual nature, still fizzing with life and excitement to the end.

Not that Wanda had much time for 'the end' as a useful way of describing this part of her journey. Despite the pain and grief of dying, she was always a joy to be with and an inspiration to others. I remember one clear example of her attitude quite near the end of her life, when we were sharing together in prayer. 'Think how much more effectively I will be able to pray for the peace of the world from the perspective of heaven' was her indefatigable response to her shortening earthly perspective, as pain and weariness closed in upon her.

Thank you, Wanda. You have now passed through the condition of 'Being Old' and used the experience to give us these wonderful insights to help us on our own journeys into God.

Your old friend,
Tim
Revd Tim Selwood, Winchester team ministry

Introduction

I was scanning the shelves of my local Christian bookshop for ideas. I wanted a speaker for a series of talks I was planning, and a Grove booklet on 'Stillness' caught my eye. It was just such simple tools for stillness that I thought busy people could do with.[1] As I approached the cash desk, for some reason, I asked the assistant whether the author of the book was local. 'Don't you know Wanda?' he replied, suggesting that *everyone* knows Wanda.

I hope this book will enable even more people to feel they know her and can benefit from her wisdom. During her life, she offered so much to many people in all sorts of walks of life—not least in stress management and inter-faith relations—and her final efforts were put into dealing with what it is to be old.

Being Old was the working title she gave this book, which was to be her final one (published posthumously now, after her death in 2015), together with excerpts from her personal journals. 'Being' rather than 'doing' was a perennial theme of hers.

Wanda wrote many books over her long lifetime and was still writing in her eighties: on combating stress (she had been a foremost stress counsellor), on faith, silence and interfaith relations, and on playfulness and prayer.

The title chosen for this, her last, book has deliberate echoes of her 1999 book *Come, Let Us Play!* because she brought the same infectious enthusiasm and curiosity to bear on her own ageing as she had done to the subject of having a spirit of playfulness when it comes to prayer. 'Our picture of God is so solemn,' she wrote. If we could be more childlike in our prayers, then our conversations with God—growing out of a certain 'playfulness which Jesus so enjoyed'— would be characterised by 'trust, abandonment, delight, gaiety and laughter'. Enjoy this book, she entreated.

Enjoyment is, partly, what I hope you will derive from these 'last words' of someone making regular entries in her journals—in small, neat handwriting and doodling diagrams—knowing that she had little time left. Yet, despite a terminal diagnosis, she maintained her *joie de vivre* to the last; she surprised us with a pink Mohican one day, even as she lost her lustrous white hair, and was determined to send me her manuscript, urging me to think whether it might be 'useful'. It is not only useful; it is pure gold for anyone coming to terms with the vicissitudes of ageing, who is wrestling with their own sense of God and, perhaps, apprehensive about how their own faith would weather a devastating blow like the news of a life-changing illness.

It is a *memento mori*, yes—a reminder that we must all die—but from someone who refused to be in any way morbid about her own impending death. She undoubtedly felt her time running out, but wanted to make sure she documented her thoughts and feelings in order to process it all herself, and to be helpful to others.

She wrote her more considered thoughts on the ageing process before the death knell of cancer, while she was still feeling reasonably fit and well. Her motivation was to capture all she wished she had known in advance, borne out of rich experience and laced with pithy, witty observations.

A friend of Wanda's told me one of his abiding memories is of visiting her at home in those last months and finding her perched on her prayer stool 'like a teenager'. 'There was a sense in which she was youthful right up to when she was very ill,' said Paul Newman, a former prison chaplain, who had met Wanda first when she went to visit prisoners at Winchester Prison. 'The moment I met her I felt I was in tune with her. She was always compassionate, wanting to be with prisoners who were among the most mentally disturbed.'

As a former broadcaster and now a chaplain myself—specifically to older people[2]—Wanda had a hunch I would both resonate with and find an audience for what she'd found to be true about this latter part of our lives: that it is a stage during which any masks we have come off; it is a time for honesty, and a seeking after what is true and what will last.

She was right. Every page rings with authenticity. It isn't a saccharine account of what it is like to lose the ability to do things we used to take for granted. I remember how Wanda would bemoan the fact her energy levels were decreasing, that she had to pace herself because, if she did too much, she'd pay for it later. She recognised her physical resources were finite, but spiritually she was only just beginning to hit her stride.

Her musings and jottings are a mixture of original thoughts and quotations from others whose writing she admired. You will find fellow authors who extol the virtues of contemplative prayer, of nurturing silence, quietening the body the better to be in tune with God.

After I had bought that original booklet of hers on 'Stillness', I tracked her down to one of her sessions in Winchester Cathedral. At the end, as others were leaving, I plucked up the courage to ask if she might come and give a talk for me (for free!). She paused, looked me straight in the eye and said, 'I shall make it *a priority*.'

I could have hugged her. As it turned out, she became a firm friend and we always greeted one another with a warm hug. Wanda left a wide and varied circle of friends. She was skilled at getting on to other people's wavelengths.

Wanda also loved riddles, puns and wordplay, parables and paradox. She was a walking paradox herself. She was one of the most action-packed women you could meet, yet ardently devoted to stillness. Someone once quipped: 'Wanda—the still small voice of calm—yet always "rushed off her feet".' She was a familiar sight on her bicycle dodging through the streets of Winchester on her way to early morning cathedral 'Stillness'. She was both 'super Martha and super Mary'.

Silence energised her for a busy life as a wife to Trevor (parish priest, then archdeacon) and as a mother, a trainer in the management of stress, a writer and a course leader on spirituality. Until latterly, she was still conducting many a course or retreat for those in need of spiritual refreshment and recreation.

It was a privilege to know her in the most active period of her life, and as she wound down. Never let it be said she wound down mentally or indeed spiritually, though. On the contrary, despite the ravages of her illness, she seemed more and more 'on fire' for God; always asking questions, puzzling. 'What on earth is he doing?' she'd cry in frustration, on occasion.

Like a dozen or so other friends, I received a handwritten letter from Wanda in her last few months summoning us to join her for silent prayer. She had been inspired profoundly by a poem from the Chilean poet and politician Pablo Neruda, entitled 'Keeping Quiet' (see p. 86). She sensed an urgency to pass the baton on to others. For, what the world needed most, she believed, was stillness and a greater appreciation of God in the silence.

A handful of times, in those last few weeks, the group we called 'Count to Twelve' (after a phrase from the poem) gathered around her bed, now in the sitting room for ease of access for nurses and oxygen tanks, and they were very precious times. She would garner every ounce of her strength to dress, kneel and direct us in prayer: prayer of the heart. These were master classes in the art of slowing down, stilling the mind, focusing on regular breathing and on paying full attention.

Wanda had always argued that stillness was 'a letting go of my need to impress myself or others, or God; a letting go of my need to strive and excel; a letting go of my need to constantly justify myself; a letting go of what drives me; a letting go of thinking about myself at all!'[3]

Of course, letting go is what each of us has to learn to do as we get older, a little at a time unclenching our fists from everything we hang on to (for grim death). Every time we succeed and let our grasp relax a little, we are rehearsing for the final letting go of our death, which Wanda firmly believed was the gateway to new life.

I have a definite sense of Wanda forging a way ahead for the rest of us who follow in her wake. Fearless in her approach, there was nevertheless a quality of innocence about Wanda, which never left her. It was not naivety in terms of human experience. She was raised in the Caribbean, in Antigua and in Fiji, among many other exotic locations, and trained as a nurse, working with Dame Cicely Saunders at St Christopher's Hospice, South London. This was a woman who travelled to Rwanda four times in the aftermath of the genocide there. She wrote *A Fable For Our Time* in 2002, an account of the brutality and torture, but also the resilience and capacity for mercy of so many of those (women, particularly) who'd witnessed the murders of their families and friends.

Transformation was her goal. Nothing less. So ageing was, for her, another part of the grand adventure of living, and her daughter Poppy and I feel she would have approved, heartily, of the defiant invitation—*Come, Let Us Age! An invitation to grow old boldly*.

Wanda is a worthy guide to a part of life—old age—which many of us remain afraid of, viscerally fearful of all that inevitable physical diminishments will bring, and its losses.

Test your mettle, though, against the confidence of a woman for whom death held no terrors. She was spared none of the side effects of the cancer, and lived with the disappointment of abandoned projects. Nevertheless, she once told me in a filmed interview, 'I can't wait to go over to the other side!' and she never demurred, however much discomfort the symptoms caused. 'I can't wait!'

Despite her fervency, there is a gentleness, a tenderness too, in her writing which permits a childlike trust. Even as she, herself, struggles (and nothing is held back in her search to be truthful, and to understand better), her words are reassuring, that none of us need, really, be afraid of the dark, the unknown.

As we share her joys and pangs, we may come to trust the silence and appreciate it as a natural, comforting medium in which to cultivate our understanding of what it is to be a truly human 'being'... even unto death.

> Be still and know that I am *God*...[4]
> Be still and know that I *am*...
> Be still and *know*...
> Be *still*...
> *Be*...

Debbie Thrower, founder and team leader of The Gift of Years

Setting the context

When my mother, Wanda, was in her late seventies, she began writing what was to be her last book. She was passionate about writing something candid yet positive about growing old from a Christian perspective. Prior to her diagnosis of terminal cancer in 2014, she had written the manuscript and was in the process of finding a publisher. She informally called it *Being old—and my take on it*. At this stage, the book addressed the limitations of ageing, but in a tone which was both poignant and uplifting. At this mature stage of her life, Wanda was well and for the most part enjoying life, alongside a growing realisation that her physical energy was decreasing with time.

This book, which Wanda originally envisaged as a chronicle of good news and encouragement for those in their older years, has given Debbie Thrower and me the opportunity to include material from Wanda's courageous and gracious struggle with cancer. Wanda's enthusiasm and zest for life, so evident to all those who knew her prior to her diagnosis, shows through even as an ageing and ill person approaching the end of her life. Throughout her illness, Wanda never stopped writing, thinking and discussing life's big questions. She had a striking combination of intellect, insight and wisdom which was apparent right through to the end of her life.

As Wanda progressed through her seventies, she became increasingly convinced (and vocal) that old age is perceived by the majority of society as something to be scorned, belittled, ridiculed, pitied, resented, trivialised, threatened by, but above all, as something to be feared and dreaded. It is no coincidence that all of these perceptions induce negative emotions and 'depressing' connotations. Indeed, as Wanda was only too aware, millions of pounds each year continue to be spent by cosmetic industries expounding the qualities of their products in reducing the signs of ageing skin, disguising greying hair, reinvigorating flagging energy levels and even flagging libido. Wanda was keen to explore the paradox gripping modern society: on the one hand, the incessant quest to look younger, and on the other, the desire to live longer, perhaps due to fear of what happens next. She found it puzzling why people wish to live longer, yet without their apparent recognition that this probably also means living with increasing incapacity and decreasing health.

Wanda, in her usual, inimitable way, wished to put the record straight. In place of all the negativity, she wanted to paint a picture of old age and ageing as she was experiencing it. Alongside the inevitable signs of diminishing energy, Wanda saw ageing as an opportunity to embrace and celebrate the fruits of life experience, the wisdom gained from coping with life's trials and tribulations, greater understanding of what it is to be human and, perhaps most important of all, the certainty in her mind that life after death was approaching ever closer. Far from actually fearing old age, Wanda was curious to see and experience what 'adventures' it would bring in its wake. It is with this conviction that the best was yet to come that Wanda set out to write her 'take' on being old and, subsequently, on being old and ill.

The third part of this book provides testament to the fact that, despite ageing and illness, life still has purpose and significance. As one of her four daughters, I feel so privileged to have shared that journey with my mother. Over the course of her illness, we shared many thoughts, ideas and discussions as well as emotions about being old and ill. I am delighted to have the opportunity to include many of my mother's insights in this book. As will become evident, I have prefaced Wanda's writings in square brackets, setting them in context and providing perspective where necessary.

Wanda had an endearing love of the quirky, unusual and spontaneous. She would have fully encompassed the lighthearted tone of the title of this book in addressing some of the most profound and poignant questions about life and how to embrace it in the mature years. Wanda thought 'outside the box'; she was an original thinker, yet she considered herself to be a contemplative, someone who actively seeks their own space and company in order to get closer to God in silence. To many, she was ahead of her time in terms of her spiritual insights, yet she was so skilled in telling the rest of us what those insights meant to her, as well as their relevance for us and the world in general. Indeed, Wanda's wisdom shines through her writing, enabling readers of every age to appreciate the gift of ageing, something to be nurtured and even cherished, rather than battled with and resented.

Rather than seeing getting older as a challenge and a threat, Wanda saw these aspects of her own life as an 'adventure' which needed to be explored, understood and befriended as far as possible.

In this book, we have taken the opportunity to draw on some of Wanda's material in her earlier book, *Come, Let Us Play!* (1999), as it exemplifies the lighthearted nature of this adventure. Indeed, far from seeing ageing as a period of increasing heaviness, gravity and seriousness, Wanda urges us on to lighten our metaphorical load and to embrace the silly, the comical and the potential for playfulness in increasing age.

As will become apparent as you read *Come, Let Us Age!*, Wanda's 'adventure' (her word) in relation to ageing and illness took her to new heights of joy and anticipation, as well as depths of despair. Wanda's deep Christian faith supported her through all this, to enable her to say on more than one occasion to those around her that she was 'looking forward to the other side'.

The following sections set out Wanda's 'take' on what it is to be old, from her original material and long before serious illness reared its head.

Poppy Nash

Come, let us age!

An invitation to grow old boldly

1

The preliminary scene

Tricky, but it happens, willy-nilly.

And you find yourself, perhaps, saying over and over:

> 'Did I get it right?'
> 'Am I any use now?'
> 'Is it too late?'
> *'Am I forgotten?'*

I'm not particularly good at BEING OLD, but I *am* old; so that is what I bring to the writing of a book such as this.

It may be you find in these pages something that can open a new way for you, a different slant to facing decrepitude—a word, rising originally from an old working meaning '*to rattle and creak*'! I hope you may find a variation on familiar words in the New Testament. If you have already found a way for yourself, reading this may open an unexpected path to offer others. I certainly don't want to turn aside and indulge in 'vain jangling' (1 Timothy 1:6, KJV), nor swerve from common sense, but either way, here goes.

This is likely to be an outrageous book by an outrageous old woman. If you do discover 'new' ways and means to tackle old age inside these pages, they are born from rage at the waste, greed and apparent futility of the place we are now in, in our present culture. Lately, as I age, there has been born in me a new sort of hope, mostly about the purpose of Old Age. Something you may enjoy too.

There is very little mention of old age in the Gospels or Epistles. We tend to think of the widow who puts in her mite as being old, but her age is not mentioned in any of our translations. Lucky old Anna was indeed old; she was widowed after only seven years of early marriage, but by this very circumstance she was enabled to live out her life in the courts of the temple, the House of the Living God. There she prayed and fasted, by day and by night. The temple staff must have taken good care of her because at the very great age (in those days) of 84 she had the priceless privilege of seeing the baby of Mary and Joseph when they brought him up from Bethlehem to Jerusalem.

The trio must have been bone-tired; it was a long journey on foot, carrying the baby, and we don't know if they had a donkey to help them. The Jewish law insisted Mary must be 'purified' and that Jesus, as their firstborn son, must be 'consecrated to God'. So, together with the necessary pair of doves, they struggled up to the Temple. Simeon, whose age we are not given, saw the baby and, unexpectedly (and shockingly!), he expressed in ecstasy the wonder of it with, *Now*, Lord, 'you may… dismiss your servant in peace!' (Luke 2:29). One look at the ten-day-old baby and he was ready to move over, into the next world. Anna simply came up to the child, praised God for him, and thereafter 'talked of him to all who were looking for the… [deliverance] of Jerusalem' (Luke 2:38, AMPC). Following all those years of dedication, self-giving and discipline, Anna had been sent a total conviction of hope, which she could spread to others. Lucky, lucky woman.

We are also told that Mary herself 'marvelled' at this extraordinary incident. A 'stopping-in-your-tracks' sense of marvel—astounded, awed. Was this the first time that Jesus, now in bodily form, experienced Stillness? All this happened in strong contrast to the appalling conditions of occupation on the streets outside the temple: there, Roman soldiers on duty might practise their 'skills' of spearing—on young people and children as they happened to pass by.

The only other direct reference I can find in the New Testament to being elderly is 1 Timothy 5:1, where we are told, 'Do not rebuke an older man; on the contrary, advise him as if he were your father' (CCB). These days the role is rather reversed; we, the elderly, presume to give the young advice, although the challenges with which they have to cope are so very different from anything with which we are familiar. Jesus himself tells us it is not practical to put old wine into new skins.

There are however some lovely references to old age in the Old Testament: for instance: 'Blessed, happy, fortunate, spiritually prosperous *and* to be envied is he who waits expectantly *and* earnestly [who endures without wavering beyond the period of tribulation]... But you [Daniel, who was now over ninety years of age], go your way until the end; for you shall rest and shall stand [fast] in your allotted place at the end of your days' (Daniel 12:12–13, AMPC).

So, if there is really so little in the New Testament about being old, where shall we start?

2

What is old age for?

Is old age really included in the purposes of God?

The following paragraph really startles me, and may well startle you too: I must proclaim my stance before going any further. I have to acknowledge where I'm at. I find that I cannot believe that God—the great God that created, and still creates, all things, cosmically and microscopically; the One that makes all things new—can have invented old age. Nothing in nature in the wild—as far as I have discovered—*nothing* in the wild either experiences old age or dies of old age. Plants 'die', in order to rest and give rebirth. Animals, if they are carnivores, die either by being eaten by other animals, or of infection and disease. Herbivores die when the food runs out, or when they can no longer keep up with their group. Many birds can survive several winters—by various means—and die when their natural bodily energy weakens, or they are eaten by larger birds. Insects have shorter lives, such as some dragonflies which die a natural death from exhaustion after 36 hours of glorious living.

Nothing in nature cares for its old. Nothing in nature encourages its old to exist longer than they can function for the good of their community. Indeed, I can find no living thing—other than humankind—that puts energy and resources into keeping old members alive once they have ceased to be 'of use' to others. Old elephants simply fall behind as the community moves on and the family leaves them to die of want. Old trees just wither, and become compost for their surrounding growth. Nothing else in nature puts up with ageing members relying on energy and time from younger generations, who themselves are vital to their community as producers. Nor does anything created demand endless and exhausting 'care' from relatives who themselves are growing older. We, today, apply 'Christian' care to old people who are beyond their practical usefulness and are emotionally depleted, and housed in scraggy, impotent bodies—with many apologies to the men and women who miraculously defy this description. But is this process actually 'Christian'?

Much of this thinking derives from a particularly special time of my life. When I was 75 (several years ago now), the Makhad Trust very courteously accepted the risk of taking me to the heart of the Sinai desert. In that vast space, with its distances of empty sand dunes and ranges of towering blocks layered by prehistoric rock formations, for miles and miles, I was granted insights that may perhaps be unusual. For several days and nights, I was fasting and in solitude, and God supplied me with his huge Solicitude. Something that lives with me every day, now. It was there that I learnt about the Bedouin practice of giving well-loved people who had died, relatives and friends, back to the desert to be recycled: their every cell becomes reused as energy for the life of other desert creatures. *Nothing is wasted.* Not one atom of body matter remains unused. Thanks be to God! At first, this was, to me, a horrifying idea, and I admit that presenting it here may horrify readers: yet, it has led me ever since to thank our God for his generous plan, purpose, provisioning for the ripening, harvesting, and *recycling* of everything he creates, throughout the animal and vegetable world.

It seems to me that it is *only* humankind that has interrupted, distracted, diverted this cycle and made it possible for men and women to live longer than they want to live, and that, simply by 'caring' for them, it disallows them to die. Antibiotics, transplants, invasive procedures are *marvellous* for those still with usefulness to others in their lives, but why do we insist on preventing someone who yearns to move over to a better life from doing what they most earnestly desire? Just to postpone, temporarily, death—which is, after all, the goal for which we work the whole of our lives. This amazing goal, promised from the moment of our 'quickening', is avoided with an unconscionable degree of energy and resources, until it actually presents itself as the final unavoidable necessity, NOW.

Have the interim time and the requisite resources and energy been usefully applied, or have they been unnecessary, in effect 'wasted'?

I realise that such questions are bestirring and challenging; but they are not to be ignored.

So, in the face of that, how useful can we—the very old—be to God? What use can he make of us?

God made us in order that we could join in with his joy and delight. How do we do this when we are old, and energy-less, and have lost our dynamism and beauty? What is there left for us to offer him?

Would he like our emptiness?

3

Would God like an empty space which only he can refill?

As bits of our brain drop off, our wits scamper away like rabbits and immediate memories spatter into nothingness—is this a tragedy or an opportunity?

> Can it be an 'exercise' that we can *choose*?
> > Might it turn into a physical, emotional, spiritual '*good*'?
> > > Clearing a space for our Creator?
> > > > Emptying, in order to be refilled by God?

To give him space in this busy and so preoccupied world from which he can operate his own purposes? Maybe it could be something like clearing the loft for modern insulation, which is a deliberate, desirable activity—in spite of the horrendous loss and back-stretching work involved. In place of the fear of growing decrepit; instead of resenting future possibilities like memory loss and being taken 'where you do not want to go' (Jesus' remark to Peter in John 21:18); rather than crying over our lessening ability to 'be useful', we can decide to make a clear area: to become emptied, so God can fill us and take over. And we can do this voluntarily!

Being old need not mean diminishment. It's a new chance to meet new learning curves and become friends with them. Opportunities abound to enliven my skills of patience, of letting go, leaving be, allowing. Things I've just skirted around before can at last become my joy, my standby, my way of getting on with those near me and indeed my very soul. All this simply depends on my willingness to taste their flavour. I no longer have to be here (and everywhere), do that (as well as this), instantly recognise and remember the tales of everyone I meet. And when my memory fails me, I can happily confess to going through a 'senior moment', because these moments are familiar to all those I spend time with now. They actually form a bond, a point of commonality! They can become times of thanksgiving too: 'Thank God, I didn't mess that one up too badly.' At those times when patience, letting go, leaving be and allowing come smoothly, there can be a new sense of being enfolded and becoming enfolding, and so others (even some unknown and unseen by us) can benefit.

4

How on earth can we do this?

We have to decide to do something about it ourselves, deliberately, individually. We're not going to get much help from other people; on the whole, they are younger than we are and won't entirely appreciate our situation. Many of our contemporaries have already moved over into the other life, the more glory-filled life on the other side. So when you can muster up the decision and purpose and will to do something about it, put aside a particular time and place for it, and try out the following practice for yourself.

For me, the most helpful position is to lie flat on my back on my bed (in the winter, I even stay under the covers), without a pillow so that my spine is straight. My arms are by my sides with hands turned up—in the position of receiving. If I'm lying on the floor my arms can be at right angles to my body in the cruciform position; but being old, many of us find getting up again from the floor can be a bit problematic!

You may prefer to sit in a straight-backed chair. It's not about maintaining a rigidly upright position, but allowing each vertebra of the spine to 'sit' on top of the vertebra beneath it, which results in the most relaxed position of all, where the spine can support itself in its favourite position, that of a lovely long 'S'.

The first thing is to tell myself, yet again, that God will supply all the energy, time and will for anything he wants me to do; everything that is in his purpose for me to undertake. God will never ask or expect me to take on anything that is outside his own will. So primarily, it's my job to get rid of everything that blocks his way. I need to empty myself of my own ideas and projects not because they are 'bad', but because they may be selfish or ambitious, over-demanding or confusing. If I can persuade myself to let all my own concerns go, I can make space for his to move in!

So, to start with, I let my head and neck stretch up towards the ceiling (or the bedhead, if I'm lying flat), and then let it gently settle back to balance on the very top of the spine.

In this position, it is easy to imagine a funnel from above passing into my head. So it comes naturally to ask God to 'funnel' his own energy into my head, into my brain and thoughts. To do this I have to make room in my head by deliberately 'dispossessing' my own ideas and thoughts. Letting them out, not clinging to them, as it were putting them into his lap. Once these are out of the way, there is plenty of room for the Holy Spirit to pour his prayer, purpose and power into the empty space. The inflowing Spirit of God takes up all the organs of communication too: he takes over my eyes and ears, my mouth and tongue: he displaces all my own thoughts and senses so that what is of God enters, and anything that is not of God is pushed out.

Then I think of this same Spirit flowing down my neck into my chest. In my chest lies my heart and with it all the feelings and emotions that are centred there. Some are very strong, and I have to work at dispossessing them (even the 'good' ones) quite firmly, so that there is plenty of space for God and his purposes to come in. My chest also contains my lungs, and I imagine God's Spirit pushing my chest out so that I can breathe in anything that is of God, and pulling my ribs back down so that anything that is not of God can be expelled: the presence of God can settle there and be carried round to every cell of my body, cleaning and replenishing every nucleus and nerve that my Creator has put there. Also, in the top half of my body is my stomach, and I imagine all that is in there being churned around and made *ready to be digested; some of it may be beneficial and some of it may be toxic—but it is all being prepared to be sorted out in the guts. Whenever I can make space there for God to come in he can sort out his priorities, and put them to work in his way.*

So, eventually, the Spirit of God enters the centre of my body, to stay there as long as I allow him. My 'guts' are frequently mentioned in the Old Testament, although the original term, 'bowels', is used more often. In modern translations it is more safely retranslated as 'inner resources'. In my guts lies the seat of my intentions, intuitions, inspirations and of my very being. There, anything that is useful is sorted out and taken into my bloodstream; anything that is hurtful or poisonous and not wanted is turned out as waste. Once again, I 'dispossess' all that is of me in my guts, and make a centre for all that is of God. Everything God-worthy is absorbed, all that is not-of-God is disposed of. Also, in my belly is the solar plexus—that accretion of nerves that sends messages throughout the whole nervous system. I especially want God's prayer, purpose, power and presence to be there.

Not to be neglected in that part of my body are the sources of reproduction—the factories of seed, either male or female, and the means of passing it to another at the right and appropriate times. Here, too, I long for the things of God to be present, and those not of God to shrivel.

Lastly, I attend to my limbs; I ask that the neural pathways, the muscles with their power to move the bones, and the ligaments which hold it all together can be filled with and powered by the things of God, and all that is not of God can be dispossessed. Then the places my legs take me to, and the things my arms and hands do—clasping, lifting, pushing, hugging, creating—should be of God, while all that is against God should go.

All of this is in order that everything in my head, heart and body should be tools, working for the kingdom of God, for the people of God, the will and power and purposes of God instead of the kingdom of me, the purposes and greed of me, the disasters and misunderstandings and hurts that I have the freedom to impose. So when I make an act of emptying myself of them and ask God to replace them with the Prayer, Praise, Power, Purpose and Presence of our great Triune God, Father, Son and Holy Spirit, it may be what God wants too.

Sometimes, during (or after) this exercise, I may feel that all the 'tools' given to me by God during my long life have now become feeble; then I just simply offer him the tool shed.

It's simple really: it's about saying to GOD: 'Me out, you in.'

None of this may appeal to you; it may simply not be your thing. But it is amazing how—given time—it can form a solid platform from which to approach 'usefulness' in being old. This sort of practice will come up again in a different form later, since it is something real and practical that we can do for God, and for the world God has put us into. Before getting into that, let's look directly at some of the immediate and obvious consequences attached to the simple fact of being old.

5

Some of the consequences of being old

'Gather the pieces… let nothing be wasted' (John 6:12)
becoming rooted
… bearing fruit

Of course, there is some Inevitable Weakening of my being, of my own familiar self. Gradually we each have to come to terms with a myriad of losses. Losing friends and relatives becomes a practical necessity as circumstances change and people I love move. Keeping contact through cards is a great asset, even though it has become so commercialised. Such exchanges reassure me I am not forgotten, and relevant 'lists' keep me from totally forgetting!

As others, now more capable than I am, take over the financial, legal, organisational sides of living, there is a great awareness that I can no longer be 'In Control'. Whether we are ever, or can be ever, 'In Control' is a debatable matter, but certainly the feeling of losing control is extremely debilitating, and can feel humiliating. So let's *give control away*, rather than fretting that it is being snatched from us. Such a relief, not having to bother with all that responsibility.

Probably bodily pain will increase in some way or other. An old friend—'old' in both senses of the word!—wrote to me she was 'aching, but still here'. So she's counting her blessings. Pain is extraordinarily powerful in reducing our mobility, and worsening our tempers. These are among the new learning curves we have to deal with, without, if possible, becoming too much of a drag on others. Some people find that they can 'offer' their pain to God; it can be part of the currency for the redemption of others, as indeed Jesus Christ offered his suffering for our own redemption. This is a high, high calling, filled with mystery and outside of logic, but it certainly works for many.

Loss of memory is a dread and a reality for most of us as we grow older. We have this in common, and can grow into a communal sense of comedy. Self-pride has to be thrown out of the window, so perhaps humility and sharing can grow in its place. Specially, I'm grateful to friends who make a point of collecting jokes about the comedic mishaps that occur—share the fun! It can help to soften the hurt; but there's no denying the hurt, too. At the beginning, any reduction in power, capacity, control is mixed up with my own sense of what makes me worthwhile to my community. The training, experiences, responsibilities I have gathered over the years: maybe these were factors in my prime, but now it is important that I learn to hand them over; to '*give over*' to those around me, to the community, to God who originally *lent* them to me. To hand them back to where they came from. Such prime qualities were not deserved, nor bought, nor endowed, but *lent*. Now I must make place for others, to contribute their ideas and conclusions, and get myself out of their way. It's my job to set about doing this with thanksgiving for what I have experienced, and hand it over, without rancour.

Some suggestions

Physical limitations

Yes, indeed, and this is always hard to take. But it would be even harder if I happened to live in a country—and there are so many of them—where wheelchairs, stairlifts, walking poles, amanuenses, ambulances, therapies of all kinds, medical and nursing and physiotherapy skills, occupational therapists, therapists and carers and counsellors of all sorts and sizes were not available. Only those who have been lucky enough to visit places in underdeveloped societies can really imagine something of the life to be endured without these resources. We do well to think on these things too, as well as the beauties that lie around us, and which don't actually depend on our own physical management.

> *A water-carrier was hired by a wise and kindly gentleman to fetch water for his daily needs from the river which was over a mile away.*
>
> *The water-carrier duly hitched two large pottery pitchers to a yoke over his shoulders, and trotted back and forth each day until his master's household was equipped with the proper amount of water.*
>
> *After a little while the water-carrier became increasingly distressed, because each trip he made delivered less water, and each day he had to increase the number of journeys he made between the house and the river.*
>
> *With great apologies and much self-searching, he approached his master with the problem: with loud lamenting he cried out, 'The harder I try, the less I bring you.'*
>
> *'Look,' said the master, 'have you noticed what has happened on the path you have taken?' The water-carrier turned around and looked at the way he had come. The master said, 'One of your pitchers is cracked and has been leaking: on that side of your return journey see what has happened.' The water-carrier looked, and see! One side of the path way was dry and cracked; on the other, there were beautiful and multicoloured flowers growing, and butterflies and bees were feeding on them.*
>
> *And all because of a simple crack.*

Holy Spirit, impassion my heart that I may give so that others have energy to spread gladness, respect and honour to those around them.

Whatever our limitation, it can give us a bit of a lift to give the muscles that do function the pleasure of exercise. Simply doing 'isometric' exercises—stretching and tensing muscles just where I am—can be re-energising. I find it fun to squeeze different sets of muscles in different patterns—they relax better and become less stiff. So instead of setting myself such goals as running or walking or swimming, as I used to do, I simply concentrate on a particular part of my body and tighten it; there is little actual movement involved and I can stay sitting or lying or standing. When, after a few seconds, they are released, the blood moves around a bit more, so I'm warmer. The same can happen with a different set of muscles. This focus and these stretches don't threaten my balance or movement, but they do strengthen and make the most of those muscles of which I still have control. Whether it's in a chair, or on the bed, or—best of all!—in a hot bath, the place doesn't matter very much; it's what I choose to do with my available muscle-power that matters.

Cerebral limitations

Depression
  Fading memory,
    lost memories
      Simple stupidity!
Remorse, particularly about my earlier mismanagement,
    ineptness, in dealing
      with *anger*—mine, and that of others coming at me.

Yes, I can beat myself up quite a lot about my past mistakes, mismanagement, misreading of tricky situations. Not a lot to be done about them now, not a lot of time or energy left. But for this moment, this now, the sense of these mistakes has mellowed a bit, along with that of my peers. So, some of the bones I used to chew on like a dog can be let go of, and left behind: they don't have to be gone over and over as they used to be; they can simply be left behind, hopefully. They don't have to be continually rehearsed, as if there was a hidden secret ability to change things.

When I'm *really* convinced I've turned out a total no-gooder, I try to remember that in Jesus' teaching and practice (which is even more pertinent) the dogs under the table were fed; and that those with blocked ears, tied tongues, those who were unwashed, lacking faith and with neither material goods nor intellectual prowess were attended to by the Son of God; they were healed, refreshed, remotivated by him; warmed, held, loved by him; called 'little children' and 'friends' by him. So there's hope for every one of us, including me, after all.

Sometimes, when thinking on these things, I can get an unannounced picture. A Jungian dream? Where it comes from, and who sends it, is not an issue here. For instance, today, during a time of Stillness,

> *I was a large, ripe, juicy apple.*
> *And God came along and took a huge bite out of the apple.*
> *I think he found it quite tasty and pleasurable, because another bite was taken, and then another.*
> *Soon nothing was left but the core.*
> *BUT within the core lay the seeds of the apple:*
> *the cause for which the apple had been grown.*
> *And the seeds couldn't get out and be spread and germinated for others*
> *unless the apple had been eaten or rotted! Then I knew what made it worth it.*

And I've found a special prayer:

> *Lord, bearing in mind all the things I've neglected;*
> *All those things of which I am ignorant;*
> *All the things I've forgotten;*
> *All the things I've lost*
> *I place them into your hands where they will be warmed and cared for*
> *so much better than if I had done so for myself.*

Moral limitations

There's always this terrible danger of 'living in the past': of trying to apply the morality and conditions of previous decades (about five of them!) to today's world, and today's understanding of the waywardness of humanity. The past was *not* 'always best'. I think of the story of the elderly son of a doctor who was bemoaning the fact that 'these days the doctors aren't worth their salt. In my childhood days my father was out every night bringing babies to birth; during the daytime he was so dedicated to his patients and gave them such care that we hardly ever saw him!'

Response: 'So the fact is that you were deprived of a loving father, and your mother was deprived of a helping husband and your father was deprived of twenty years of his life—isn't it better that now these have been restored by modern working conditions?'

Obviously, some of the moral behaviour taken up by young people today is difficult for an older generation to accept easily. Sometimes our anger may raise its head to cover up a rather sneaky jealousy at their apparent 'freedom'; maybe we could actually rejoice that we never had the need to be besotted with brand names, obsessed with make-up, impelled to look up the latest post on Facebook, or be engaged by Twitter, or have to carry all the boy-band members' names tattooed on our hearts.

Thank goodness I am left now with the ability to be on my own and to positively enjoy personal privacy. The conversation and observations of others are a fascination for a time, but oh! the release of being left on my own for a while!

The following is derived from a poem I was given years ago by Jeanne Blowers. It goes like this:

> To SONbathe is to allow the lightening ray of God to shine in your
>   soul;
> It is to rest in depths too deep for thought, and heights too steep
>   to climb;
> It is to gaze in adoration, to loosen oneself in the radiance, open
>   to the holy hue
> And (although you know it not), some will find
> The Grace to Sonbathe too.[5]

Sexual limitations

Of course; what to do about SEX? The fantasies and yearnings remain; not so many opportunities, perhaps, and more subdued arousal—but it's still very much around. Flirtations can still be fun, and the ability to draw in is great; but where on from there? The emotion and memory last perhaps a bit longer than the action. Testosterone and oestrogen still perfume the air, but lovemaking itself is more effective in words than with nerve endings. In former days there was much more going on in bed, probably, but that left little time for reflection and the caring choice of phrase, or even depth of 'emotional intelligence'. Now, wordplay can mean as much or more than foreplay did in earlier days (and nights). And that's a cause of multiple thanksgiving, if not quite multiple orgasms. And much less exhausting!

Protest limitations

In one's own personal climate the times for large public protest are over. But in the small domestic climate, chances for sudden irritable protest abound. Is this one of the new challenges? Continual irritable protesting and self-defending can be the cause of ruination to a steady loving receptive relationship, so something has to be done to curb them. It needs barrow-loads and barrow-loads of acceptance (*not* protest) of the other person's capacity—or the dwindling of it—and of my own (*and the dwindling of it!*). And the ordinary process of accepting also involves appreciation. So, barrow-loads of acceptance, appreciation and patience. And because of his great mercy God will supply these, too, if I empty my own will of protest. One way could be something like this—and the great advantage of being old is that time is so much more malleable! Usually, there is so much more of it, and that's a great help.

It came to me quite recently during a time of Stillness that has helped me, personally, a lot. My reduced and withering being was in front of me, and not unnaturally I was saddened by it. Then I discovered that there were three 'slits' in the image: one in my forehead, one in my chest, and one in my belly. These 'slits' were well disguised and quite difficult to see, but if one of them was pulled out it came attached to a sloping chute, rather like the old way of depositing cheques into the bank. And nearby Jesus was standing with a shovel, waiting to shoot great dollops of Grace and Guidance into the opening.

Great dollops of Grace and Guidance into my brain;
　into my heart;
　　and into my guts.
　　　How favoured was I?!

Remorse

Remorse for the past: compunction, yes, but not 'guilt'. Guilt has such a strange history. Firstly, it is a word *hardly ever used by Jesus*! It's fascinating to rummage through the Gospels and find only a few mentions of 'guilt'! Repentance, yes, lots and lots of calls to repentance. Forgiveness—even more of this. The adjective 'guilty' is rarely used by Jesus, depending on the translation. I could only find two references to it: firstly, referring to the one who is 'guilty' of sinning against the Holy Spirit being beyond forgiveness (Mark 3:29), and secondly (in some translations only), when the woman caught in adultery was brought before him. His response then was 'let any one of you who is without sin be the first to throw a stone at her' (John 8:7)—and they all moved away.

Sometimes 'remorse' itself can be turned into simple grief for past events; for the loss of companions and opportunities; for the remembrance of tenderness and generosity of those who have moved on, among many other memories; then we simply have to turn it into thanksgiving that we knew them at all.

There are times, of course, when the black dog of depression and regret and realisation of my own reduced capacity pulls me right down. I remember my own hurtful use of ill-considered remarks; my unkindness and misuse of the sensibilities of others. I'm really no good and never have been and have done nothing to alleviate the weariness of this world. What was the point of me being alive at all? Perhaps I shouldn't even have come.

And then, out of the blue, the Gospel in church includes that extraordinary tiny parable, the one seldom highlighted or repeated. It's about the contrast between Judgement and Redemption: it is only recorded by Luke, who pops it in between a heavy description of important historical events, and some enormously significant Sabbath healings (Luke 13:6–9). Why?

> The story tells of a man who owns a large vineyard, and his frustration at the fruitlessness of a fig tree, standing in the middle of his estate, which has not produced fruit for three years. He tells the gardener to cut it down.
>
> But the Gardener replies. 'Give it one more chance,' he says. 'I will dig all around it and add more manure: just see if it responds. Cut it down next year if there is still no fruit.'

With everything else he had to attend to, the Gardener was prepared to give this one little tree another chance.
And I, even in my present state of worthlessness, am as important to Jesus as that!

Dependence

So often our prized independence has to be given over to Dependence: 'when you are old you will… [be led] where you do not want to go' (John 21:18). But aren't I lucky to have people around me to take me where I am safe (even though I may be sorrowful), warmed (if not by my own fireside) and fed (even if it isn't with food of my own making), by such reliable others?

Added to this, I'm just beginning to realise that a lot of me is dead already. No longer can I count on the verve I used to have of making every second fulfilling; no longer can I rely on the gift of immediate perception I used to have. I'm told I still think quickly, talk quickly, move quickly; but I can no longer reach into where other people are so instantly. As my stock of energy—of every kind—gets less, my social contacts are narrowing, my intellectual interests are fewer, my involvement in areas outside my own life are disappearing. So, it becomes more important than ever to make the most of *this* moment *now*; it's not so much about disentangling what got me here, as about what can be done with *now*.

Thinking about what got us here is pretty useless: it breeds arguments and accusations and distraction and worse. But it's such a great advantage to learn to let go of the need to explain and prove; to give up the urge to pull the other down, to show up their mistakes and to be 'in the right' myself. It's much more simple to concentrate on where we are at, on where we have arrived, *now*.

Simple regret

I'm sad I no longer reply instantly to my correspondents and contacts—very dear and important ones; some are in Africa, for instance, or Japan, or Australia. I no longer manage to get away for a day a month to a solitary place; books don't get finished; gardening is no longer an urgent passion, nor is sex. I've got to cut away my deep desire to be involved with a lot of aspects of my daughters' lives, and instead concentrate on the lives of my elderly husband and ailing older sister. If I can make their lives easier, that is undoubtedly 'a good thing'. But in order to do so I have to accept shaving away other things, and let them die in me. They themselves are probably in that process anyway, so better to acknowledge it! I'm glad Paul talks about dying to self and rising to glory; 'as dying, and, behold, we live' (2 Corinthians 6:9, KJV). Jesus was keen on that theme too.

Eventually, there comes a time where such 'limitations' bring me to the point where I have to face an obvious FACT: that I have reached a stage of life that is different from any other; the three basic drivers that underlie every earlier part of my life are no longer required, no longer useful, no longer of any help to either myself or others.

These three basic drivers are to be able to tell others:

- what I *want* to do—this is now very seldom appropriate and no longer particularly interesting;
- what I think they should acknowledge that I *know*—what they know is of much greater significance in their care of me;
- and—perhaps most important of all—that *I am right*

I have now reached the stage when none of these are *applicable to me*.

So, once again, I have the chance either to grumble and complain and make life a misery to those around me, *or* to choose to give up these earlier priorities voluntarily, and thereby free up time and energy to enjoy the wants, the knowledge and the rights of others

Then, in all probability, I will be treated with kindness and concern.

The Bible has a lot to say about deliberately giving things up; I especially like the reference to Moses as one who 'by faith... left Egypt, not fearing the king's anger; he persevered because he saw him who is invisible' (Hebrews 11:27).

Of course, the process of leaving such significant drivers behind is difficult, and it can hurt. But then, I have to remind myself that Jesus Christ chose, voluntarily, to be crucified.

That makes all the difference.

Some *additions to my being*

More time

Yes, tasks take longer, but when demands are fewer there logically *is* more time. It may even be the last time. May I live as if it were! If this is the last time, may I use it with the warmest of my abilities.[6]

More gratitude

It's my turn now; my turn has come for others to take responsibility—that's what they have grown up for: to carry their own choices and decisions. If I can allow myself to do what they want me to do, I will be all that much less of a burden to them. And every kind word, every glance at beauty, every generous suggestion, every moment free of pain is a chance to express gratitude: aloud, or just to God.

More time to breathe

Being old, breathing can become less taken-for-granted, less unconsidered. It can become difficult, painful, at times excruciating. But this of its own gives us the chance to be more aware of the different mechanics of taking breath in, and letting it out. It is, of course, what keeps us going at all, but for most of our lives most of us take it for granted, not using it as helpfully as we can. Medical professionals seldom have the time available to teach the most productive ways of breathing, although in some countries there is an established professional resource of Breathing Therapists. This is not the place to expand on this amazingly useful subject, but readers are encouraged to seek out help from sports therapists or speech therapists in this country. In dire cases patients are, of course, supplied with oxygen, and drugs to calm tight muscles, relieve tension, loosen fluids. But being old necessarily involves some greater consciousness of breath, of 'normal' breathing. 'Short of breath' becomes common; cold air means 'taking in a sharp breath', but so also does amazement, fright, and inspiration.

Becoming conscious of a deeper, slower way of drawing air into the lungs using *only* the soft abdominal muscles (no stiff joints to move, no heavy bones to shift up and down, no direct involvement of the heart muscle) and learning to let it go slowly and calmly can be an enormous boon.

Choice

Okay, there may, on the whole, be less choice around for me personally as my own activity lessens, but how we all loved in *Fiddler on the Roof* when Topol sang, 'On the other hand…'; 'but then, again…' There are always alternative ways of approaching a problem, with different turns and alternative viewpoints to be explored. And this is my chance to learn them!

Some philosophers decry our claims to have much *choice* anyway, and we have to accept that to a large degree our genes and our conditioning do frame our imaginations and creativity. Nevertheless, there remains that small segment of opportunity where we can use a degree of choice, as we discussed earlier. Wherever there is choice, there goes with it a degree of control over the choices of others. It's quite startling to realise that:

> *Even when I am 'giving', I might be using it to 'control' the other;*
> *when I'm deliberately 'not choosing', maybe I'm hiding from the blame that might go with my choice;*
> *I can choose to control by denouncing;*
> *or I can choose to control by boosting and complimenting.*

Some choose to control by 'this is the way';
is it the only way?

One of the 'strengths' of being older, less active, is that I can choose to let go of control.

So, when there is time—perhaps when I wake early and the house is quiet and undemanding—I lie flat on my back without a pillow, and have my arms loosely held away from my sides. I become aware of all the jobs, worries, intentions I have for the coming day. Then, deliberately, I press my head against the mattress as hard as I can, and feel the tension in my hard, unrelenting skull and at the back of my neck: caused by all these demands and stresses. Very consciously and very deliberately I dispossess them, and let them go—into the waiting hands of God—leaving my cranium empty. When I then relax my neck I can wallow in the looseness and calmness that freedom from stresses brings.

Next, I deliberately hunch my shoulders up to my ears, and make myself aware of the tension and discomfort of trying to bear all the burdens I fancy are put upon my shoulders—either placed there by others or taken on by me. Then, I pull my shoulders down, deliberately and consciously dispossessing the burdens, letting them roll off my sloping shoulders, letting them go—into the waiting hands of God—and relaxing into that freedom.

Thirdly, I roll my hands into tight fists, clenching them, grasping and gripping the tasks expected of them today (after all, I am the only one who can do them properly, it's my duty). Then I carefully unroll my fists, opening out the palms and spreading the fingers so all those 'doings' can roll away: I dispossess them and let them go—into the waiting hands of God—and become aware of what he can do with my emptied hands.

Next, my feet. Pulling my toes up towards my knees, I think of all the places my feet will be carrying me to today, how painful and tired they will get. I realise that I feel I am the only one who can discharge those duties, and how burdensome they are. Then, consciously and deliberately, I dispossess them, and let them go—into the waiting hands of God. My feet are freed up to do what God wants of them, not what I impose on them.

Crucially, I next attend to the central part of my body, the area to which all these other parts are attached. The central part that encases my heart, the centre of my feelings; my lungs, the centre of my breathing; my stomach, the centre of my food intake; and my guts, the centre of my whole body, where all that is useful and good gets absorbed and becomes useful, and where all that is waste and useless is got rid of. It's also figuratively thought of as the centre of my deepest 'knowing', my intuitions and 'gut-hunches'. I realise the pain caused to me and others if any of these parts dysfunction. And, then, deliberately and consciously, I dispossess and let them go—into the waiting hands of God.

This area was mentioned at the beginning of this book, and continues to be the most telling part of my being.

Finally, I become conscious that God alone knows his will for me today; God alone can put into action whatever he plans and purposes for me today; and God alone will supply whatever energy is needed for that particular part of his will. So I can entirely trust to him to supply at the exact moment the right amount of physical energy, mental empathy, wit and emotion to apply to that particular episode, in the way that he would have it discharged.

So, I can meet the day and whatever it brings lighter, emptier, more receptive and open and perhaps even with a bit of eagerness to see what happens.

Getting closer to when I can 'move on'

Why do we hear so little from our spiritual leaders and advisers about looking forward to, welcoming in and longing for that Other Side?! Sometimes it feels as though there is a conspiracy of silence about the matter within *all* religions.

The time is inevitably shortening before I am actually in the place of Marvel,

- where all my questions will be answered;
- where I shall be understood better than at any time I have spent on earth;
- where, perhaps, I shall comprehend why I was created in the first place, and whether I have accomplished whatever it was that I was intended to attempt;
- where I shall find out whether anything I have ever done has brought the kingdom of God closer to the time when 'the earth shall be filled with the Glory of God as the waters cover the sea';
- where I shall rejoin my preceding relatives and friends (in whatever form they have taken now); and where I shall be exposed to as much of the full glory of God and God's joy and merriment as I am able to be;
- from where I can 'look down' on this world and pray more heartily and effectively for its common good;
- where the 'have-tos' and 'ought-tos' melt into 'desire to' and 'want to' for the sake of the kingdom;
- *and* where, of course, I can join in the general fantastic party that is going on in heaven!

HEAVEN
the ONLY PLACE where we can *let go, let it all out*; where we can get out of the shackles of constraint, and control, and convention; where we can get from what is expected of us; where we can come *face to face with the Lord of Wildness and Amazement, Play and Surprise.*

A really beautiful old lady I used to visit in residential care used to say:

> It's nothing to do with staying alive: the staff here do everything possible to keep me alive. The problem is, how to get dead!

Clearing the loft: handing over; 'passing on'

Those readers of this book that are of my generation will be familiar with the phrase *'Get a grip'*. Get a grip on yourself and your negative emotions. Get a grip on your job; get a grip on your confusion.

I fail when I 'lose my grip' on life. Fear of loosening our grip on things is something that comes to all of us as we grow older; yet here we are discussing the advantages of 'loosening my grip'! Such an extraordinary, countercultural suggestion! Is it God's will? Putting aside our deep and fundamental desire to be 'in the Right' and 'in the Know'?

The ancient problems of suffering, loss, disability, misfortune have challenged philosophers for centuries, and numerous scholarly tomes have been written in the effort to explain why 'doing our best' doesn't necessarily bring ease to our lives. Maybe such questions go on eternally, until we come to that amazing place where I shall 'know even as also I am known' (1 Corinthians 13:12, KJV), and *all* questions will be answered. When I was just five, this was the reason why I decided to remain a Christian and it's still very potent for me. Recently I came across the following:

> *A butterfly is one of the most beautiful things in this world, especially one from the tropics.*
>
> *It spreads its wings, glowing, glistening, shimmering in the sunshine—all to the glory of God.*

To the glory of God, yes, but also it has to find a mate. Eggs are laid, and the eggs turn into caterpillars: caterpillars that eat my cabbages! But if my cabbages weren't eaten, there would be fewer butterflies!

So if, for ourselves, we can 'loosen our grip' on our own personal expectations of our capacities, we can free ourselves up to try something different. The same sort of freedom and loosening of ordinary expectations applies to our prayer life too. We can invent our own way of approaching God, using quite different and unusual forms of words, such as the following:

Turning to God

At the beginning of the Week of Prayer for Christian Unity, we'll use the term *Gospodi*, which is the name for our Triune God, Father, Son and Holy Spirit, found in the Russian Orthodox Church.

Gospodi
Being Uncreated—
Supreme God of all there is,
We approach in vast Awe and Wonder;
You know all things: there is nothing not known by You
Our divisions and different traditions are known to You
You understand why these divisions have arisen,
and You know the inner being of each of us, through and through:
In jubilation, we honour You

Lord, we ask You to be with all those who work in the field of
knowing, the use of knowledge:
those who teach or are taught:
those who train, or are trained,
those who lead or are led.
As experts advance bearing a great deal of knowledge,
be with those who feel they are without knowledge.

May those who have it refrain from implying they have it all;
and those with less be enabled to value what they have.

Gospodi
Creator of every thing
There is nothing You do not see
Nothing hidden or in shadow
All is exposed to You and Your gaze.
In jubilation, we thank You.

Lord, be with our inventors and innovators;
the men and women who bring about change;
those who research and create;
those who tackle the waywardness of mankind,
and the ways of the natural world.
Guide those who hold power, Lord, for change,
but most especially support those who feel powerless.
May innovation and change be directed
in all ways towards Your Kingdom,
O God and Father of us all.

Gospodi
Designer of all sounds
There is nothing unheard by You, nothing misunderstood;
Lord of the sound waves
In jubilation, may we listen to You.

Lord, be with those who think they have heard it all,
and are in the Right.
Those who may have forgotten *to listen*.
They may be financiers, or politicians,
managing directors or even clergy,
but they may also include war-mongers:
All those who are certain they've got it Right,
and impose their Right on others.

Most especially Lord, we pray that the aims of war
may be loosened towards closer
cooperation with neighbouring nations;
and may the great tide of new reforms develop smoothly,
with the least offence and bloodshed.

Gospodi
You are the Word, the source of all words,
all savourings and touchings;
You comprehend the hurts and the cries, the truths and the lies
the tryings and the fallings-short
that occur within any communication;
You know and fully understand the strongly held beliefs
that result in division.
But You also sort out the love and the offerings,
the caring and the sharing,
the delight and the joys:
In honest humility,
we plead for Your anointing of all who reach-out to You,
Place Your touch on each one You have created.

Lord, in today's world we are bugged
not only by unwise communication,
but also by too much communication.
We can become confused and self-defensive,
in our families, in our churches and communities,
and in our national policies.
Then sometimes we even unlearn what is Best,
and replace it with self-regard and greed.
Great God, help us to listen to You,
to widen our knowledge of Your precepts,
and deepen our comprehension and
compassion towards Your world.
Be with those who work to better our education, health,
security and understanding of each other.

Gospodi
Being beyond all human beings
Being over immensity—and over microcosm—
Different and Other: without boundaries, without limits,
—only bits of us can relate to bits of You:
And yet sometimes we find we can jubilate
in the very freedom of Unknowing.

There are times when we are troubled by the sick,
the desperate, the tortured,
the confused people in our world;
those who feel useless and unwanted;
those without homes and without jobs.
Lord, we bring them to You, high on our hearts for Your Touch.
Especially, we pray for those who have asked for prayer
but also we pray for those who do not ask,
nor know how to ask, for our prayers.
We carry on our hearts those who have recently lost their lives,
whether through illness, conflict or accident,
or even by their own intent.
Be with all who are in pain, fear, or grief,
and help us to remind them and their loved ones,
that 'Underneath are Your everlasting arms'.

Gospodi
You know, see, hear and touch
anyone or anything that turns towards You
Burn in us; glowing and radiant,
and crumble to ashes ALL You find that is *Not of God*.
Or perhaps better still, using no words at all, simply 'basking'!

6

Some conclusions about being very old

I am totally convinced that Being Old can be USEFUL. God *does* have a purpose for us, of course. Many Old People are a fund of experience, wisdom and stories. But even for the very ordinary common or garden old person, we DO have a function.

For so many in our secularised society, behaviour is simply about getting where and what they want to get. Doing what suits them. Motive, intention, furthering-the-kingdom-of-God hardly bears upon their choices or decision-making. Contributing to the common good seldom comes into it. So it is all the more important that those of us who yearn for the coming of a better world know that every single action or thought or intention we have actually furthers it or hinders it, and increases the power and creativity of the total Good or the accumulated evils: the fundamental principles and 'powers' that inhabit our world, and are 'at war' in the highest places of the spiritual world. So, every time we can include a good intention or a bad intention into our thoughts or responses or actions or yearnings, it adds either to the capital of Good or to the total of evil in our planet.

'Evil', as a separate entity of its own, is a subject that today is almost taboo to talk about. I sometimes wish that just as we have Capital letters we can use to aggrandise a name or noun, it would be good to have an opposite system of demoting a name or noun. If the initial letter were made smaller, rather than larger, then I could refer to the adversaries, the opponents, the other side, the poles apart.

Words like 'devils', 'demons', 'Satan' personify satanic powers, and I'm not so keen on doing that. But, importantly, as we grow older we have better opportunities to quite deliberately spend time and prayer to diminish these forces—so clearly acknowledged by Paul— to deflate them, put them down, tell them to *scram*; to tell them we don't want them, they don't belong, to shove off. In thinking of those in trouble, of course, we pray that God may increase his influence and purpose, but equally as old persons perhaps we are less inhibited in demanding that his opponent should get his claws out of, loosen his teeth from, remove his grip on, let go of the one for whom we are anguishing. As I understand it, addressing the opponents of God in this way was acceptable in medieval times. Is it something we have lost and in these times it is crucial to remember?

And yet, and yet, and yet
The Kingdom of God is WITHIN YOU and ME!

TOTALLY AND UTTERLY ASTONISHING

As you will know, there are mountains of scholarly works which discuss the 'whats and wherefores' of the kingdom of God. I lost count of Jesus' own references to the kingdom in the Gospels (quite apart from those in the Acts and Epistles) at 88! Among other images which Jesus Christ used when speaking of the kingdom of God are good wheat seed, a mustard seed, yeast, treasure hidden in a field, a pearl of great price, a coin, a dragnet, a little child, a landowner with labourers, a king who gave a feast, wise bridesmaids and drinking new wine with his Father.

Paul speaks of it as power, glory, righteousness, peace and joy.

AND Jesus said that all this is within you and within me!
How privileged, and un-frightened, and loved, and safe can we be?
And yet, and yet, we all have to '*Abhor self-righteousness*'!

As we get older, and perhaps more aware of our own depletions and pains, it becomes all too easy to fall into the trap of 'nobody understands' and 'it's not my fault, so I am owed'.

When we feel we have spent a long life doing our best (it's easy to put out of our memories the times when 'my best' wasn't enough!), a particular sort of self-protection and self-righteousness can set in, even though we may be quite unaware of it. We perhaps don't believe others when they try to point it out. It certainly happened (happens) to me. On a certain day, at a certain time, I yearned for release from this truly devilish spirit of self-righteousness that had taken hold of me: I asked for it to be seared and torn from my ailing heart. As a penultimate thought to this present brief account of what it is like for me to BE OLD, I'll leave you with this extract:

Christ is ALL and IN ALL

Therefore, clothe yourselves with tender-hearted pity [heartfelt compassion] and mercy; kindly feeling, and generosity, a lowly opinion of yourself; humility and meekness; gentle ways and patience.

Bear with one another tirelessly, with endurance whatever comes, with good temper and good humour.

The Lord has forgiven you, now you must do the same.

Over all these clothes, put on LOVE, and enfold yourselves with the bond that binds everything together in divine harmony. At all times be THANKFUL, appreciative, giving praise to God, and making melody in your hearts.

COLOSSIANS 3:12–16 (paraphrase)

And you'll never feel again that your life no longer holds a challenge!

Do we HAVE to be afraid of Death? Or is it just such a Huge Release— into the Unknown perhaps, or maybe through a secret gateway into something hugely greater than we could ever have imagined? Some people actually long for death. Dying may indeed be unpleasant and very difficult, but at the end of dying itself there is such a startlingly new and mysterious country to be explored! Jesus Christ called himself 'the Living Water', and John builds on this to describe 'a pure river of water of life, clear as crystal, proceeding out of the throne of God' (Revelation 22:1, JUB); and similarly in front of the throne is 'a sea of glass like unto crystal' (Revelation 4:6, JUB). After this murky, muddied and muddled life, isn't that just what we will all be looking for? *And can be looking forward to?* 'I will give unto him that is thirsty of the fountain of the water of life freely' (Revelation 21:6, JUB).

One of the best things for me is that such explorations, mysteries, discoveries will not be available to me on my own, but the whole company of heaven will be beside me too. Sometimes, when I go into Winchester Cathedral very early in the morning and am the only person in that vast nave—the longest uninterrupted nave in Europe—it feels as though the whole gigantic space is stuffed to the brim with past kings and queens, saints and scholars, sophisticates and peasants, erudite and pastoral, public and private personages of all shapes and sizes and status and health, jumbled together like black-eyed peas in a pot, every one of them praying and hoping and thanking, every one of them with one thing in their sight: the glory of God their Creator, all down the ages. And all that is a miniscule model of what happens in heaven. I can join them, if I am chosen; unless I choose for myself to turn my back on them and disbelieve them.

I long to taste the air of the Other side, as yearningly as the lover longs for the Beloved in the Song of Songs; as achingly as Mary the Magdalene yearned to touch her Lord in the garden— an enveloping desire to get closer to the heart of God than is manageable in this frenetic world. To be there where I can pray for others with more effect than I can here; to be part of the on-going sweep of the purposes of God. But until that marvel- filled day dawns,

I know I must passionately submit to Being Alive.

Jesus, our beloved Lord and Redeemer, our Helpmeet and Friend and Model, is recorded as frequently foretelling of his own death; he forewarned his friends without rancour or embarrassment; when 'his time' had come, he proclaimed it and deliberately '*chose*' both the timing and the method. Having done that, he was silent and put up no defence or delaying tactics whatever; he simply stuck to his purpose of fulfilling the prophesies and his Father's will.

Come, let us play!

A grown-up term for play is 'heuristic' creativity; in other words, self-discovery through play. In one of her books, *Come, Let Us Play!* (1999), Wanda explored the playfulness not only of children but also of God. She invited adults to rediscover their playful natures as a way of tapping into an aspect of God we tend to neglect, if not overlook entirely. Here are some pertinent extracts from that book.[7]

7

God laughing

There are rare occasions when people are given a profound glimpse into the glory and closeness of God laughing. Sometimes an experience is given that infects everything else experienced in life thereafter. One such incident, reported by a woman who was on retreat, occurred while she was walking in the woods in silence. She heard, 'Sit on my shoulder as a young child does, and I will show you wonders you have never conceived.' Jesus carried her as he and she went through his whole life, laughing and laughing; and even in his passion there was submerged laughter in the strength of his confidence and hope. It changed her entire perspective on God for the rest of her life. A similar experience came from a priest working in a downtown area. He described it in personal correspondence. During an individually guided retreat, this man meditated upon the question Jesus put to the blind man (Luke 18:35–43). 'What do you want me to do for you?' He dared to reply, and his prayer was answered. He writes:

Wow!! Joy!! Laughter!!!!—and he LAUGHED, LAUGHED uncontrollably, to such an extent he literally fell over with laughter! He experienced what Irenaeus meant: 'the glory of God is a person fully alive'. *This must have been how the woman with the haemorrhage felt when she was made whole! Cartwheeling for joy everywhere—'the rejoicing with unutterable and exalted joy' (1 Peter 1:8, RSV). And I caught a glimpse of Heaven! Alleluia!!*

His life and prayer were changed. There was exuberance and exaltation all rolled into one.

8

The magnitude of God

In playfulness, I can sometimes break through the barriers of magnitude and awe that separate me from God. For instance, look at this:

God is great and unknowable.

His knowledge and wisdom are unfathomable, unapproachable, a vast distance away from our puny understanding.

Think of the grains of the sand on just one beach. Imagine building a cube of sand one foot long, one foot wide, and one foot high. Imagine the number of grains of sand in that one cube.

Make the sandcastle one yard by one yard by one yard. It's very big; there are multitudes of grains of sand in that castle, unimaginable numbers. Let your mind wander over all those granules.

Extend the castle to *five* yards by five yards by five yards. What sense can be made of numbers now?

Think of one *unique* grain of sand in the bottom left-hand corner.

That *one grain* represents Earth, a star in one universe that God has created.[8]

And that God loves me.

Now that is something to laugh about.

Personal reflection

- To arrive at that place where I can get lost in wonder, love, praise and play, I have to feel safe. Lion cubs, puppies, young children only play where it is *safe*. Am I safe with God? Or is he still a judgemental Father to me, and do I still have to cringe before him? He has said he wants to call me 'friend';[9] do I insist on still being a slave?

- He so often laughs back at me in my prayers—when I get it incongruously wrong and he lets me know that *he* knows it all, I don't. When I get too bumptious by half—he gives me an appropriate put-down, just as he did to Peter when he was too impetuous.

- At those times when I get too big for my boots, thinking my way is so much better than the way of the person I'm not getting on with, God reminds me that he loves that one quite as much as he loves me, and he chuckles about it.

- The only possible response is that of the loved child: to respond incredulous with playfulness, thankfulness, and abandonment into the arms of God. And then *I know* that

  if I fail, God still loves me;
  if I get the wrong end of the stick, God will still love me;
  if I make a hash of things, God still goes on loving me
  (maybe I will feel it is more difficult to hear his voice, I have
      stepped backwards,
  but God continues to love me, because he can't help it, he
      is Love);
  if I turn away from him, he continues to love me;
  if I fail to own him, or even deliberately betray him, God will
      continue to love me
  (maybe others will find it difficult to see God's light in me, but
  it is I who will have hidden it);
  if I remain unhealed, God loves me even more;
  when I am wounded, vulnerable, receptive, his love has
      no bounds
  because it is unfettered by my competence.
      Praise to him in everything.

Every time I want to leap and dance in his presence, he will leap and dance with me; holding me, holding on to me, releasing and catching me, twirling me with an exchange of freedom and intimacy, closeness and letting go. Safety and risk rolled into one; assurance and challenge mixing and twisting. I am leaping into his welcome.

9

Alongside the pain and the hurt

Behold, thou desireth truth in the inward parts: and in the hidden part thou shalt make me to know wisdom…

Make me to hear joy and gladness; that the bones which thou hast broken may rejoice.

PSALM 51:6, 8 (KJV)

If thou hast no liking to meditate on My Passion with weeping eyes because of the bitter agony I suffered, then meditate on it with a laughing heart, because of the joyous benefit thou will find in it.

Henry Suso, a fourteenth-century mystic[10]

Poetry and Hums aren't things that you get, they're things that get you.

Pooh's Little Instruction Book[11]

Precedents

Lewis Carroll, Spike Milligan, Lionel Blue, Norman Cousins, Marti Caine, Michael Bentine, Tony Hancock, John Cleese, Brian Keenan and John McCarthy[12] are a varied collection of people, and there are many more that could be added to them. What they have in common is that they all declared publicly that they intended to get through their troubles—and these were varied enough—by means of play and laughter.

These people affirm an extraordinary paradox: that tragedy can be borne more hopefully when playfulness is present.

In its turn, to be authentic and grounded, playfulness must be aware of tears. The way of a God-filled life is like a dual carriageway of pain and delight—but there are many crossover points. It is a parallel path: to share with others our pain, and to share with others our delight. There are times to show how we hurt, and others to expand our joys, even the small ones. Can pain be touched by playfulness?

Love needs love in return; delight needs to be delighted in; just so, suffering needs recognition and at some level it needs to be shared. But there is a basic difference; love and delight can be mutual, but the sharing of pain can only be partial. The one who is alongside the pain of another can genuinely 'feel for' the hurting, but only rarely can they dive to the same depths. Strangely enough, the bridge that links them is often a sort of playfulness. Here is a moving example of how this can happen.

In his book *Iris* (Abacus, 1999), John Bayley describes the last illness of his wife, the philosopher and novelist Iris Murdoch. She had a particularly distressing form of Alzheimer's disease. Right through the book, his infinite and tender form of waiting-care never wavers. It is made all the more poignant because a near-playfulness keeps breaking through. Bayley is discussing how 'teasing' seemed at times to relieve his wife of her vacancy and despair. He continues:

> All this sounds quite merry... and I try to seem to explain the trouble. The Alzheimer face has been clinically described as the 'lion face'. An apparently odd comparison but in fact a very apt one. The Alzheimer face is neither tragic nor comic... [it] indicates only an absence. That is why the sudden appearance of a smile is so extraordinary... Only a joke survives, the last thing that finds its way into consciousness when the brain is atrophied.[13]

Right in the middle of deep pain, an echo of ridiculousness lifts it. And in that moment others are included.

10

Feeling awful and playing

In our anguish, for ourselves or for others, we long for a type of relief that is obvious and positive and overwhelming; what we discover is that comfort often comes in the shape of hints and whispers, rustlings and even chucklings. It is about a subtle, ingenuous and sometimes incongruous exchange. The awfulness that others are going through can indeed fill us with awe, but that in itself distances us from being alongside them. It can reinforce the 'crossing the road' syndrome. Coming along this less definable way, sometimes we can approach the hurt and the hurter a bit more positively even though we fumble at it. There are four angles to note:

1 When I'm feeling awful, a mere touch of playfulness may prevent me from 'awfulising' what is already bad enough. A close friend described it recently: 'When things get that bad, the only resort you've got is laughter.' The word she used is interesting: it's not about a holiday resort, but it hints at a new sorting out of priorities, a *re-sort*.

2 When I'm feeling awful, the sharing of laughter or play or empathy may open up something which has previously been closed tight. A hug, a stroke, a giggle can begin to prise apart the prison bars which have been holding back all sorts of negatives. Perhaps at that stage they can be met by a good chortle *with* them, though never *at* them. Crying with people when they want to cry is natural and empathetic; on occasion, an alongside chuckle brings relief of a different quality.

3 Children are particularly good at showing the way this is done. Staff who work in hospitals or hospices have at their fingertips scores of stories about sick children and playfulness. Most of them retain the zig-zag path between pain and playfulness right up to the final stages of their illness. Jane Grayshon writes particularly sensitively about this.[14] She quotes one child putting it like this: 'Pain is a feeling just like gladness but pain is much sadder than gladness'; and another who says, 'If people didn't have pain that would mean a big feeling was missing; even though it would be good to be happy all the time, it wouldn't be right.'

4 Many elderly people manage to hang on to a similar twinkle in their eyes, even though they are chronically disabled. A twinkle that redeems us all, the one in pain and those alongside them: it closes the gap, and it wipes out anything akin to resentment or self-pity. There are those who have progressive or terminal illness and who describe their super-awareness of the play and enjoyment in life.

To cap the evidence of this difficult terrain, there is a remarkable woman from Rwanda. She saw her husband, sons, parents and siblings tortured and killed. 'I have been condemned to live,' she said, in a matter-of-fact sort of way, 'but I'm going to make sure that I am *alive-alive, not alive-dead.*'

11

Jesus and optimism

What about the attitude of Jesus? Jack Dominian, the renowned psychiatrist, has tried to analyse the roots of Jesus' attitudes in his life on earth. He says that while Jesus had:

> the capacity to feel the inner world of others, [he still] showed optimism in his approach to disease, which he felt could be conquered, and to his own suffering, which he was convinced would not overwhelm him. Ultimately, he was also optimistic in his awareness that death is not the end.[15]

This 'capacity to feel the inner world' means being aware of need in myself as well as in the other, then owning it, whether it is in me or another, instead of hiding from it or disguising it. It is allowing authenticity and absurdity to hold hands over it. It is about the hurt child in Jesus coming out running to meet the hurt child in me with arms wide open.

12

Jesus and his needs

This is something to stop us in our tracks in wonder... It is almost thinking the unthinkable. The Gospels show that Jesus, in the full likeness of God, opened up to us *his own need*. There are times when this is the way God himself engages us. (Can we bear that prospect and still stay mentally stable?) Here are some instances:

- Jesus Christ, even as the face of God, told his disciples of his need for rest in their company.
- Many times he told those who were in pain he needed to know what they wanted of him.
- He told those around him he wanted the children near him.
- He engaged the woman at the well in Samaria by telling her of his thirst.
- He engaged the men who had tortured him, scoffed at him, driven nails into his hands and feet—by telling them, too, of his thirst.

Jesus, although he was the Son of God, was a real, pulsating, needing human being. God makes it easier for us to tell him of our needs, by letting us know of his.

God asks us to join him in his need; he even asks some rare people to be alongside him in his incalculable grief. John Taylor puts it like this:

It is God as Self-Giver who expresses himself continuously in the spontaneous, uncompelled outflow of love for his people. His is the pure will, that at whatever cost to himself, they should be there, and a pure delight in their being there whatever the outcome. Because this God fulfils his divinity in inexhaustible self-giving, his delight is the fierce joy of the artist or the mountaineer that persists unabated by any amount of real pain, anger or defeat. His is the bliss that can include and outshine all suffering.[16]

God, in his outpouring love, feels the pain of the world as we do but multiplied incalculably. And yet his delight in the world must be greater. As John Taylor again pointed out, *the delight has to be greater than the pain or he would annihilate the world.*

13

Being pierced, but still being welcoming

This is one of the deepest mysteries: that the sword and the welcome fit together. It is to do with the concept that the present piercing experience is somehow bound up into one with the invitation to play with God. I can be available to playfulness, even while I am hurting or disadvantaged or 'challenged' or feeling less-of-myself-than-I-could-be, then something transforming and miraculous happens.

Maybe this is the heart of Christlikeness; maybe it is this that makes Christ-centredness unique among the great world religions. We believe that God asks us to hold the invitation and the welcome at one with the sword. It is a first priority to relieve pain and suffering, but at the core where it cannot be removed, Jesus Christ modelled a way of extending love and play to all who would listen. In his own life he acted out the claim that the 'good cheer' he repeatedly offers us is greater than the pain. He did so to convince us that, whatever may happen, 'all shall be well, and all shall be well, and all manner of thing shall be well'.[17]

Personal reflection

This amazing grace of holding pain and hurting and still being sufficiently open to welcome playfulness cannot be contrived; it can only be prayed for. It cannot be forced, but it can be received. It is something much more than what is rather vaguely called 'a sense of humour'. When it's there, it is a gift direct from God.

This is very personal, but other people will talk of very similar experiences. It happens only in the depths of stillness. At some rare and unforgettable times, when wrestling with a real distress, a deep gurgling rumble is felt at the centre of the body. It is in the place where still prayer is most centred. It erupts with a total conviction of the trustworthiness of God, and it bursts up and out in a freeing, unbinding laughter that explodes the bonds of despair. Its roots are the love of God and his incomprehensible ability to turn all things around for good. The Celtic invitation 'Come, Mary's Son, my Friend, our fullness is in You' is the consequent outburst. I am left convinced I need to *invite* God ever more profoundly into my life.

> May the cross of Christ be over this face and this ear
> May the cross of Christ be over this mouth and this throat
> May the cross of Christ be over these my arms
> From my shoulders to my hands.
>
> May the cross of Christ be within me, before me;
> May the cross of Christ be above me, behind me.
>
> With the cross of Christ I meet
> Every difficulty in the heights and in the depths.
> From the top of my head to the nail of my toes –
> I trust in your cross, O Christ.[18]

Extracts from
Wanda Nash's journals[19]

14

Being old and ill: where is God?[20]

[I remember, even in the throes of illness, Wanda conveyed a real sense of anticipation and even delight at the prospect of life after death. She was a master of wordplay, as evidenced in her search for meaning in the following extracts from her journal.][21]

What is the sole thing that ONLY MY SOUL CAN OFFER?

IT MAY BE this will be *the most important section of my whole life*! Not about what I do, say, write, perform. *All* about being in tune with
WHO ART IN HEAVEN—
THY KINGDOM COME
THY will be done
Emptying, channelling, praying CONSTANTLY;
offering and accepting—*without being 'cross'*!

[Wanda's courageous attempt to make sense of her illness as a Christian believer is articulated in the following excerpts. They collectively explore some heart-searching questions, which Wanda poses in conversation with herself and with God, in seeking clarification and guidance from him.]

STRANGE! I've got a whole set of brand new priorities: an entirely 'new' bunch of priorities to do with matters of the SPIRIT—the God-loving inner core of each of us.

How do I use it?
Who for?
Who to share it?
Is it shareable?
How can this new 'vision', this new sight/site, increase Glory to God?

✢

How to express it? My sole aim at this present is to tease out what God *really* wants of me, how I can best serve him, please him, in these last days/weeks/months of the life he has so marvellously lent me. How can I begin to make up for all I have sidelined during my wonderful life? Is there any possibility that anything of *me* can make better anything of anybody else's?

✢

TWO QUESTIONS:
Q: What does God want me to do?
A: Be peace-full and peace-able.

Q: What has your faith done for you?
A: HELD ME UP!

✢

[Having posed these soul-searching questions, it is as if Wanda has found some resolution, some clarity and purpose, some answers from God himself. She continues with a more confident voice, full of conviction and faith in God.]

WHAT HE WANTS
is absolute,
un-reasoning,
TRUST…

MYSTERY
not knowing
not understanding
not making sense.

⁜

GOD ALLOWS '*UNCOMFORTABLE THINGS*', THOUGH NOT TO TEST US,
BUT TO TEACH US!

⁜

Every description,
every adjective and adverb limits him,
our limitless, indescribable GOD.

⁜

EVERY ATOM OF BORNE, UNCURSED SUFFERING CAN BE *USED* for the
purpose of God, but only while it is uncursed.

15

Awareness of
God's presence in illness

[Alongside Wanda's search for meaning in her illness, she found immense and continual comfort in the knowledge that she wasn't alone. She had a real sense of God's presence, which supported and guided her through her darkest hours. The following extracts from her journal offer a glimpse of the comfort to be gained from an awareness of God's presence in and through illness, and the need to trust in God's presence at all times.]

Even tho' the day be laden
and my task be dreary,
and my strength small,
a song keeps singing in my heart.
For I know that I am Thine;
I am part of Thee.
Thou art kin to me
and all my times
ARE IN THY HAND.

Hebridean prayer transcribed by Alistair Maclean,
from *Waymarks* (Northumbria Community)

✛

The Living Rhythm (sometimes 'unbearable') that *supports* art, taste, movement, hearing, poetry, friendship, invention, music, gardening—chatting, even cooking and eating, learning, climbing, and on, and on, and on... *IS ALWAYS THERE*... You only have to listen!

I have a little house:
'Tis the house of my Soul

And there I live and move
In the house of my Soul

I do not live alone
In the house of my Soul

God lives along with me
In the house of my Soul

When it's quiet as a mouse
In the house of my Soul

When I am very still
In the house of my Soul

God speaks sometimes to me
In the house of my Soul

And then I speak to him
In the house of my Soul.
Fay Inchfawn[22]

I am lying down with God the Father who
created me, and knows me inside out.

I am lying down with God the Son who
experienced all there is in the world.

I am lying down with God the Holy Spirit
who breathes into and out of everything.

[And on a lighter note, a play on words][23]

JESUS IS NEAR
NEVER FEAR!
JESUS IS HERE
'ERE, 'ERE

16

Using illness: ministry through illness

[Having grappled with the search for meaning in her illness and having found great solace in the presence of God, it is as if Wanda then finds inner strength to use her illness for Christian ministry. That is, in Wanda's journal, she devotes much space in the later stages of her illness to what she can do in furthering God's kingdom on earth, as the following excerpts suggest.]

Precious Lord—You understand
and share 'suffering' so well—
my own pain and discomfort are
getting worse—PLEASE LET ME
USE THEM productively!

Including allowing others to
Comfort and solace me!

THE BIG WORDS
Not about *me*—about *God's* work:
No, No, No crying—my ambition has been taken up by God
and carried!
My ambition—to be as close to God as he will allow me;
to add to his whopping prayers my minuscule ones,
and to deflate all non-God intentions.
The world is *GOOD*; GOD'S PLANS ARE *GOOD*,

But so much worldly wisdom obfuscates them!
At the feet of my Father (wherever he wishes for that) may I be
a de-fuser,
a de-clouder,
a de-mister—
With the *greatest possible* LOVE.
WHAT AN INVITATION!

✛

SUPPLICATION

GOD OF ALL PATIENCE—
So patient with me—
May I pass it on.
GOD OF ALL FORBEARANCE—
Such forbearance with me—
May I pass it on.
GOD OF ALL UNDERSTANDING—
Such understanding with me—
May I pass it on.

[Wanda modelled a Christian journey which not only embraced her progressive illness but also sought to maximise what she could still do for other people. In essence, Wanda's deeply held wish to serve others never left her.][24]

Think often of God, by day, by night, in your busyness and even in your diversions. He is always near you and with you, and *leave him not alone*. You would think it rude to leave alone a friend who came to visit you: why then must God be neglected? Do not then forget him, but think of him often, *adore him continually*, live and die with him. THIS IS THE GLORIOUS EMPLOYMENT OF A CHRISTIAN—if we do not know it we *MUST LEARN IT*!

[Wanda included the following ancient Hebrew prayer in her journal. This prayer clearly indicates that the journey of life may include illness, not as a barren period but as one which can bear its own fruit as a meaningful and spiritual personal 'adventure' with God. This sentiment is echoed in Wanda's own prayer which follows it.]

The Journey of Life

For each of us life is like a journey.
Birth is the beginning of this journey,
and death is not the end but the destination.
It is a journey that takes us from youth to age,
From innocence to awareness,
From ignorance to knowledge,
From foolishness to wisdom,
From weakness to strength and often back again,
From offence to forgiveness,
From loneliness to friendship,
From pain to compassion,
From fear to faith,
From defeat to victory and from victory to defeat,
until, looking backwards to ahead,
We see that victory does not lie at some high point along the way,
but in having made the journey, stage by stage.

An ancient Hebrew prayer[25]

Every experience is a
Learning experience,
and every learning experience
is a LOVING experience
and so Creator and Created grow
closer and closer.
PRAISE HIM!

17

Coping with illness in order to use it

[Wanda's journal bears testimony to her gratitude to God for life, even life with terminal cancer, as evidenced in the extracts below.]

Thank him, thank YOU, for the use (for 80 years) of my beautiful, wondrous body. The places it has taken me to! The experiences it has enabled for me! The sights, sounds, expressions, impressions it has interpreted for me! Thank you, thank you. THANK YOU, O MOST GENEROUS GOD—AMAZEMENT—AMAZEMENT.

Oh! Let It Come On.
Jesus Christ: You are the song of my soul
You are the soaring song
You are the sorrowing song
You are the serene song
You are the saving song of my soul
Yours is the smiling, seeking, sympathising song
Lord Jesus Christ, may I sing your song.

[In stark contrast to Wanda's drive to write and record her experiences of being old and ill, she also derived immense spiritual comfort from times of meditation, contemplative prayer and silence. Her insights into the power of stillness are evident in many of her writings, such as the following poem she wrote while ill.]

Stillness

'Stillness' is about emptying myself of 'me'—as far as possible,
and replacing the selfishness,
greed and competition that has settled there
with the grace and courtesy, wisdom and good cheer,
mercy and compassion of GOD by him and for him.
And God, in his MERCY, goes on carrying out this purpose
in spite of my own repeated failings.[26]

[In talking to other people about the importance of silence as an essential part of relationship with God, Wanda drew on the writings of Mother Teresa of Calcutta, especially the following prayer.]

We need to find God

We need to find God and
He cannot be found in noise and restlessness.
God is a friend of Silence.

See how nature—trees, flowers, grass—grow in Silence.
See how the moon, the stars, the sun, how they move in Silence.

Is not our mission to give God to the poor in the slums?
Not a dead God, but a living, loving God.

The more we receive in silent prayer,
the more we can give in our active life.
We need Silence to be able to touch souls.

The essential thing is not what we say,
but what God says to us and through us.
All our words will be useless, unless they come from deep within.

Words which do not give the light of Christ
increase the darkness.

Mother Teresa of Calcutta[27]

[Wanda found great solace in the verses of Psalm 119, in thinking about the need for silence in today's busy world, as her notes on a section of the Psalm illustrate.]

> I call with all my heart: answer me, Lord,
>   and I will obey your decrees.
> I call out to you; save me
>   and I will keep your statutes.
> I rise before dawn and cry for help;
>   I have put my hope in your word.
> My eyes stay open through the watches of the night,
>   that I may meditate on your promises.
> Hear my voice in accordance with your love;
>   preserve my life, Lord, according to your laws.
> Those who devise wicked schemes are near,
>   but they are far from your law.
> Yet you are near, Lord,
>   and all your commands are true.
> Long ago I learned from your statutes
>   that you established them to last for ever.
>
> PSALM 119:145–152

Each of the sections of Psalm 119 follows the Hebrew alphabet. If we are to witness to Christ in today, where there are constant demands on our *whole* person, WE NEED SILENCE. This section, 'Qoph', speaks of a mature response to dependency and prayer in difficult circumstances. The soul cries out to God and waits in silent dependency on HIM.

If we are to be always available, not only physically, but by empathy, sympathy, friendship, understanding… WE NEED SILENCE. To be able to give *joyous* unflagging hospitality, not only of house and food, but of mind, heart, body and soul, WE NEED SILENCE.

[Having been told after her summer diagnosis that she might only have a few months left to live, Wanda was a little surprised to be able to participate in New Year celebrations. The start of the new year (2015) heralded another period of deep soul-searching as to what God wanted her to do with the time she had left. About this time, my sister Phoebe introduced Wanda to a poem entitled 'Keeping Quiet' by Pablo Neruda. This poem was to play a major role in the next few months. It can be found in English in Pablo Neruda's *Extravagaria*.[28]

With hindsight, being introduced to this poem was a particularly significant moment for Wanda in her quest for meaning and clarity. Indeed, I was with her when, having read the poem over and over again, she felt called to compose a letter inviting twelve close friends, including Debbie Thrower, to join her in starting up a group which focused on 'Being quiet'.]

> ... *something strange happened to me a couple of days ago and it won't let me go. Out of the blue I was given the enclosed poem [entitled 'Keeping Quiet']. Since then, there have been constant God-nudges, with Him saying 'So Wanda, what are you going to do about it now?' So what if a few fellow-feeling friends got together occasionally simply to pray for more 'Quietness' in our world today?*
>
> *Coincidentally(?), many of the books I've come across recently describe and deplore the rush, noise, competitiveness and speed that rule our lives today, smothering all experience of 'BEING' in contrast to 'DOING'. After all, we were created to be Human Beings—not Doings!! Researches are pointing up the threats that are rooted in restlessness but affect the whole world, including nature with humankind.*
>
> *What if we were to meet now and again, simply to plead together for... 'QUIET'—and all its associated values and outcomes. Perhaps a dozen of us, so simple and yet crucial to the developing needs of our whole world.*
>
> An extract from that letter, dated 22 January 2015

[Wanda's invitations were met with a warm response from all recipients, and late in January at Wanda's bedside the 'Count to Twelve' group was formed. This group met on a regular basis over the next five months while Wanda was alive, and has continued to meet after her death.]

18

The best is yet to come

[Wanda's deep, unquestioning conviction that there is life after death is almost tangible. In conversing with her about death and dying, I actually felt her sense of anticipation and even excitement as she exclaimed: 'I can't wait!' It was as if, on dying, she was just slipping through a veil and would be waiting for us to join her sometime in the future. On various occasions, Wanda described to me insights that she had experienced, vivid images of God, as illustrated in the following excerpts.]

Two power-inducing images—tho' both so incomplete!
1 *God as magnet*: pulling us, drawing us, enticing us toward HIM…
2 *God as fragrance, perfume*: attracting us, inviting us, intriguing us into getting closer… to HIMSELF.

IN BOTH GOD IS CONTINUALLY SAYING:
COME CLOSER
'I HAVE WHAT YOU WANT'
'I AM WHAT YOU WANT TO BE'

[One of the most poignant and powerful of these insights occurred on the eve of Wanda's 79th birthday. It is particularly poignant as Wanda referred to it in detail in her Christmas 2013 letter giving family news, just months before her diagnosis of terminal cancer.]

Wanda's highlight

[Wanda's highlight? Without doubt, her last-before-becoming-eighty birthday (2013).]

It was on the same day as an annual charity event for the Homeless, where 'young' people are invited to sleep out on the Cathedral Green; instead of risking the bad weather, a 'birthday party' of us slept inside the Cathedral itself. It turned out to be an unforgettable and very profound experience which, for me, will set the tone of the next decade. The icing on top of the cake was an experience that went like this:

In the context of the many threats to the flourishing of our world we have had this year

Something Happened:

We were sleeping on paving stones, among them 900 years of graves and memorials. At 2 am, I awoke and found the whole space, from floor to the tip of the vaulted roof, peopled by a throng of those who had visited, been remembered or been buried there: a vast crowd of them. Some 'ordinary' souls and some 'saintly', and they were thrumming a hum all around us.

Then words took shape: 'Yes,' they were saying. 'Look—we lived with plagues and famines, natural disasters and wars, trials and betrayals… but now we are all together, in harmony and Peace;

'*Whatever* the troubles are, the final state is halcyon togetherness and tranquil bonding;

'At the very heart of God; from here we are praying for and supporting your world…'

Who wouldn't be excited? They said it must be shared, so here it is!

19

Finale

And *ultimately* there will be that last letting go, giving away, giving back of all our miraculously designed tools to their Designer; with the hope and prayer that they have been used on this earth to his purpose and glory: the final act of giving of my self and gratitude of my soul.

Although, in the end, we all paddle our own boat. We can lead each other, or tow each other, bump each other, wave to each other—but we each steer our own boat through the gate and over the WHAT'S THIS WORD?—

AND THEN THE GREETING

'… all shall be well, and all shall be well and all manner of thing shall be well'
Dame Julian of Norwich

[Wanda found great comfort in the following poems.]

Growth

From my birth to the present time,
there is a clear straight path.
Everything I thought deviation,
Everything I counted as unnecessary,
Missed, Wasted, Foolish, is a part of
that straight path.

> I see that an infinitely loving God has
> used every thread of my life to weave
> a perfect fabric of truth.
> Don't ask me how.

Joy Cowley, *Aotearoa Psalms*[29]

And that will be heaven

and that will be heaven

and that will be heaven
at last   the first unclouded
seeing

    to stand like the sunflower
turned full face to the sun   drenched
with light   in the still centre
held while the circling planets
hum with an utter joy

    seeing and knowing
at last   in every particle
seen and known   and not turning
away
    never turning away
again

Evangeline Paterson[30]

Notes

1   Wanda Nash, *Simple Tools for Stillness* (Grove Books, 2005).
2   Anna Chaplaincy to Older People is named after the widow Anna who, with Simeon, appears in chapter 2 of Luke's Gospel. Both were faithful older people who believed God's promises. Anna went on to speak of redemption to all who would listen. They are good role models of lives lived trusting in God. Anna, we know, was steeped in the spiritual disciplines of prayer and fasting. See thegiftofyears.org.uk.
3   Wanda Nash, *A Fable For Our Time* (Christians Aware, 2002).
4   'Be still, and know that I am God' (Psalm 46:10) was frequently used as an exercise in stillness by Wanda in this way.
5   From Jeanne Blowers, *The Call to Surrender*. Used with kind permission.
6   Wanda coped with her illness by living in the present, mindfully. I remember how, on many occasions, we agreed that the best way forward was to take a day at a time. My mother would then recommend taking not just a day at a time but an hour or even a minute at a time, as no one knows what the future holds. In a very real sense, Wanda embodied mindfulness and treasured every minute of life, however pleasurable or distressing that moment might be. This approach to coping with the unexpected became encapsulated in our mantra to live 'step by step'. This approach also chimes with Jesus' teaching in the New Testament to not be anxious about tomorrow (Matthew 6:34). We don't need to know more than a step at a time if we trust God to show us the way ahead. Wanda's understanding and living out of this biblical teaching was an inspiration to all around her, not to fret or worry about what tomorrow holds.
7   The following material is taken with permission from Wanda Nash, *Come, Let Us Play!* (Darton, Longman and Todd, 1999), pp. 72–97.
8   Derived from information heard on BBC4.
9   See John 15:13–15 (also 21:5; Luke 12:4). Some translators have used the word 'guest' in this context.
10 Henry Suso (1295–1366), *The Little Book of Eternal Wisdom*, chapter xiv. Quoted in *A Dazzling Darkness*, edited by Patrick Grant (Fount, 1985), p. 221.

11 'Inspired' by A.A. Milne (Methuen, 1996).

12 See particularly the place of humour as an antidote to despair and degradation in Brian Keenan, *An Evil Cradling* (Vintage, 1992).

13 John Bayley, *Iris* (Duckworth, 1998), pp. 44–45.

14 Jane Grayshon, *In Times of Pain* (Lion Publishing, 1990).

15 Jack Dominian, *One Like Us* (Darton, Longman and Todd, 1998), p. 66.

16 John V. Taylor, *The Christlike God* (SCM, 2011), p. 175.

17 A claim made several times throughout Julian of Norwich, *Revelations of Divine Love* (1373) edited by Dom Hudleston (Burns & Oates, 1952).

18 Attributed to Mugron, Abbot of Iona from 965 AD, quoted in *Celtic Daily Light*, compiled by Ray Simpson (Hodder & Stoughton, 1997).

19 The prospect of adding material to the existing manuscript clearly pleased my mother as she started a journal documenting her thoughts, prayers, poems and reflections on her journey through illness. From the outset, my mother's approach to her illness and the courage she showed in coping with her increasing incapacity was an incredible witness to God's abiding love and care.

20 Wanda's whole perspective on her life-restricting illness was determined not by asking 'Why me?', but rather, 'Why not me?'

21 Poppy Nash's comments appear in square brackets throughout the book.

22 Every attempt has been made to seek the location for permission for this poem, but without success.

23 Wanda's sense of humour and sense of the absurd helped us all to cope with the increasingly distressing situation we were witnessing. For example, there was laughter in the number of pills Wanda was required to take each morning and evening. Her nightly ritual of trying different ways of disguising the unpleasant taste of those pills brought shared amusement as she became increasingly creative. There was also laughter in experimenting with the best way to arouse the carer's attention in the night, while she was sleeping in the bedroom downstairs, and in exploring the different gadgets available for heightening the volume of Wanda's increasingly weak voice, as well as how best to get out of the bath.

24 Poppy Nash's sister Lois makes the following observation about our mother: *I always knew what a devout Christian Mum was ever since I was a very small child, but it wasn't until after she died that I fully appreciated how every spare minute she had—outside family, bringing*

up the children and her work—was spent on reading the scriptures/
holy books and making notes on any aspect that had made an
impression on her.

25   From *Gates of Repentance* © 1978, revised 1996 by Central
Conference of American Rabbis. Used by permission of the Central
Conference of American Rabbis. All rights reserved.

26   Another significant way in which Wanda coped with her situation
was by expressing her love and gratitude to those who visited
her and who shared her journey. This was all part of her 'mindful'
approach to being old and ill. Poppy Nash's sister Lois has
encapsulated this experience in the following comment: *I will never
forget how, the nearer to the end of her life our mother was, and the
more ill and frail she became, the more she expressed her love for
us. I can only think that God's love was just pouring through her the
nearer to death she became. Perhaps that's how she remained so
convinced the best was yet to come. Our mother had such a strong
sense that God was there for her to face whatever she had to face in
her earthly life, otherwise how could such a frail, weak body express
such powerful love? It really was too much to bear at times. Sometimes
it was overwhelming and made me feel totally unworthy.*

27   Reproduced with permission from the Mother Teresa Centre (www.
motherteresa.org).

28   See Pablo Neruda, 'Keeping Quiet' from *Extravagaria*, translated by
Alastair Reid (Farrar, Straus and Giroux, 2001).

29   From Joy Cowley, *Aotearoa Psalms* (Catholic Supplies, 1989). Every
attempt has been made to seek permission for this poem, but
without success.

30   Cited by Janet Morley (ed.), *The Heart's Time. A poem a day for Lent
and Easter* (SPCK, 2011) in the Reflection for Easter Saturday. Every
attempt has been made to seek the location for permission for this
poem, but without success.

The Gift of Years

Resourcing the spiritual journey of older people

BRF's The Gift of Years programme aims to equip churches to support older people wherever they may be – in residential care, congregations, in their own homes and in the community. At the heart of The Gift of Years is a growing network of Anna Chaplains.

Find out more at **thegiftofyears.org.uk**

 brf.org.uk